FAR
PIANO
VOCAL
GUITAR

ONE HIT WONDERS
OF THE
'50s & '60s

ISBN 0-7935-5049-1

HAL•LEONARD®
CORPORATION

7777 W. BLUEMOUND RD. P.O. BOX 13819 MILWAUKEE, WI 53213

CONTENTS

Alley Cat Song   Bent Fabric
#7 September 29, 1962   Jack Harlen, Frank Bjorn

Bent Fabric may sound like the name of a '90s alternative-rock band, but it is actually the stage name of Danish jazz pianist Bent Fabricius-Bjerre. Born in 1927, Fabric was a musician and bandleader by the time he was a teenager. He is known as the artist that recorded what are claimed to be Denmark's first jazz records. Fabric's career reached into many areas of the entertainment industry. He became the head of Metronome Records in 1950, hosted a popular Danish television show, and wrote songs under the pseudonym "Frank Bjorn." In addition to scoring #7 as a single, the album "Alley Cat" also scored on *Billboard's* top pop albums chart. "Alley Cat" won a Grammy for Best Rock 'n' Roll Record in 1962.

Angel of the Morning   Merrilee Rush & The Turnabouts
#7 June 29, 1968   Chip Taylor

Merrilee Rush joined her first band at age thirteen. She performed with the Aztecs, Merrilee & Her Men, and Tiny Tony & The Statics before settling with The Turnabouts. The Turnabouts consisted of bassist Terry Craig, drummer Pete Sack, guitarist Carl Wilson and saxophonist Neil Rush. Paul Revere saw the Turnabouts perform and decided to feature them on Raiders tours, which led to fairly steady bookings on Dick Clark's *Happening* '68 TV show. Songwriter Chip Taylor, famous for the tune "Wild Thing," originally penned "Angel of the Morning" with the voice of singer Evie Sands in mind. Sands recorded it on the Cameo label, but the company folded before her record was released. Despite scoring a #7 hit and a million seller with "Angel of the Morning," The Turnabouts didn't last long after "Angel." Members of the group did resurface within the music industry. Carl Wilson went on to form the band White Heart with sisters Anne and Nancy Wilson. They later shortened the name to Heart. Terry Craig made a career as a studio musician in Los Angeles. Merrilee Rush continued singing, issuing an album in 1982.

Apache   Jorgen Ingmann & His Guitar
#2 April 3, 1961   Jerry Lordan

Danish jazz guitarist Jorgen Ingmann made quite a sight decked out in full American Indian regalia and war paint for the "Apache" promo shots. Born in 1925 in Copenhagen, Denmark, Ingmann was playing with Danish violinist Svend Asmussen when the opportunity to cut a few singles came along. Ingmann's recordings made it to the United States thanks to Bent Fabric, a Danish jazz musician and head of Metronome Records, who arranged for Atlantic Records to release recordings by Danish musicians in the U.S. "Apache" was originally planned as the flip-side to "Echo Boogie," a number Ingmann wrote and felt would give him his American break. Ingmann was not the first to record Jerry Lordan's "Apache," a snappy tune without lyrics. British musician Bert Weedon first recorded it, and The Shadows recorded a version of the tune that sold well throughout the world but never made the American charts. For reasons that no one understood, "Apache," complete with Ingmann's zinging guitar licks, took off like wildfire in the U.S. Ingmann never toured the U.S. and although his follow-up recording "Anna" hit #54 on the pop charts, he never scored another U.S. hit.

Jorgen Ingmann
Apache

Theme from "Baby, the Rain Must Fall" Glenn Yarbrough

#12 May 22, 1965 Elmer Bernstein, Ernie Shelton

Glenn Yarbrough, Lou Gottlieb and Alex Hassilev first found success as members of the folk trio The Limeliters. The group came together via a coffeehouse Yarbrough owned in Colorado Springs called the Limelite. After the group split up in 1964, Yarbrough struck out on his own and almost immediately scored a hit with "Baby, the Rain Must Fall," the theme for the Steve McQueen and Lee Remick film of the same name. Unfortunately for Yarbrough, his middle-aged, middle-class looks did not fit the hip folkster image of the mid-'60s. Although he recorded a score of albums following his hit, nothing else really caught on. In the late '80s Yarbrough re-formed The Limeliters with Mike Settle and Gottlieb's son Tony. The group resumed touring and recording.

The Birds and the Bees Jewel Akens

#3 March 20, 1965 Herb Newman

The fact that Jewel Akens was born a boy didn't change his mother's mind. Having chosen the name Jewel for the child she was sure would be a girl, she was determined to use it. Born in 1940, Jewel was singing in a Texas church choir by the time he was eleven. When his family moved to Los Angeles, Jewel and buddy Eddie Daniels put together a group called the Four Dots. Akens did a little recording with the Four Dots and as a duo with Daniels. Jewel can also be heard on the Astro-Jets classic doo-wop recording "Boom a Lay" with a B-side of "Hide and Seek." Herb Newman, one of the founders of Era Records, gave "The Birds and the Bees" to Akens. Newman had actually written the tune under the name Barry Stuart, one of several pseudonyms he used. Several of his tunes had scored successes prior to "The Birds and the Bees," including "The Wayward Wind" and "So This Is Love." Akens continued to record after his #3 hit with "The Birds and the Bees." Although fairly successful, he never managed another hit.

Bobby's Girl Marcie Blane

#3 December 1, 1962 Gary Klein, Henry Hoffman

Marcie Blane is the perfect example of a star manufactured by the music industry. Blane graduated from high school in 1962 with no intention of pursuing a career in music until she was contacted by Marv Holtzman from Seville Records. Holtzman suggested that she record "Bobby's Girl," capitalizing on her sweet, innocent appearance and demeanor. Her songs were a hit with teen girls in the early '60s, and have found a niche in recent years with collectors. She recorded several other songs including "Little Miss Fool," "What Does a Girl Do?" and "Why Can't I Get a Guy?" All of the tunes followed the theme of her naïveté and meekness. Three years after her hit with "Bobby's Girl" Marcie Blane disappeared from the music industry. Now married with children, she works as an education director at a New York theater.

Book of Love   The Monotones
#5 April 21, 1958   Warren Davis, George Malone, Charles Patrick

The Monotones was a group of six young men that sang in four-part harmony. The group members began their musical career in a church choir that included such pop luminaries as Cissy Houston, Dionne Warwick and members of The Sweet Inspirations. Pals from childhood days in the Newark, New Jersey, housing projects, Warren Davis, George Malone, Charles Patrick, Frank Smith and brothers John and Warren Ryanes took their act to *Ted Mack's Amateur Hour* in 1956. The group put together a demo and soon Mascot, a subsidiary of Hull Records, released "Book of Love." When the tune became popular Argo Records took over national distribution. Between their touring schedule and the fact that they had made no plans for the "Book of Love" success, they had no follow-up release, and by the time they pulled together another record it was too late to cash in on the popularity of "Book of Love." After a few more releases that didn't catch much attention, the group split up. The Monotones continued performing at oldies shows for decades.

Chantilly Lace   Big Bopper
#6 November 3, 1958   J.P. Richardson

Jiles Perry ("J.P.") Richardson, known to fans as the Big Bopper, was one of the first martyrs of rock 'n' roll. Richardson died with Buddy Holly and Ritchie Valens in the crash of a small plane near Clear Lake, Iowa, on February 2, 1959. The Bopper was a successful D.J. who was a pop star in his spare time. His radio career began while he was still in high school, when Richardson assumed the on-air persona of the Big Bopper and began working for station KTRM in Beaumont, Texas. He stayed at KTRM for the rest of his life. After cutting two country and western singles under his real name, he cut a novelty record entitled "The Purple People Eater Meets the Witchdoctor." On the flip side was the rockabilly tune "Chantilly Lace" with which he would become famous. He released a couple of singles following his hit and put together a stage show that led him to the ill-fated Buddy Holly tour in 1959. Richardson returned to the charts after his death by way of "Running Bear," a song he had written for Johnny Preston.

The Deck of Cards   Wink Martindale
#7 November 2, 1959   T. Texas Tyler

Television audiences know Wink Martindale (born Winston Conrad) from his highly visible role as the host of several popular game shows including *Tic Tac Dough* and *Last Word*. Wink's career began on radio at age sixteen and continued when he became the host of the Los Angeles show *Teenage Dance Party* on KHJ-TV. "The Deck of Cards" was written and first recorded by T. Texas Tyler in 1948. The song, which is actually spoken, not sung, tells the tale of a lonely soldier and his deck of cards. Although Wink had tried his hand at recording in the mid-'50s and later released a few follow-ups to "The Deck of Cards," he found his niche elsewhere in the entertainment industry.

Dominique   The Singing Nun

#1 December 7, 1963   Soeur Sourire, Noel Regney

Soeur Sourire (Sister Smile), better known to Americans as the Singing Nun, was indeed a nun. In 1963 Philips Records agreed to record Sister Luc-Gabrielle (born Janine Deckers) and several other sisters from a Belgian convent singing a collection of original songs. The tunes, which had been hits at youth retreats, were recorded for use within the convent. When the tunes did well in a test of the European market, Philips released an album by Sister Sourire in Europe. The album *The Singing Nun* and the single "Dominique" were then released in the States. After the album and single hit #1 on the American pop charts, the Sister appeared on *The Ed Sullivan Show* and released a few more singles. Audiences, however, had lost interest and the Sister disappeared as quickly as she had appeared. Sister Luc-Gabrielle eventually left the convent to pursue a musical career on the "outside." She released a highly controversial recording of "Glory Be to God for the Golden Pill," an obviously pro-birth control statement. In 1985, after a series of hardships, the former Sister Luc-Gabrielle and Annie Pecher, her companion of 10 years, committed suicide.

Eve of Destruction   Barry McGuire

#1 September 25, 1965   Philip F. Sloan

Although Barry McGuire's name has been associated with many successful music ventures, including The Mamas & The Papas and The New Christy Minstrels, "Eve of Destruction" was his only hit as a solo artist. McGuire found the song after rejecting a number of tunes offered to him by Trousdale Music. He heard songwriter Philip Sloan playing a guitar and asked him if he had any new songs. Sloan played him "Eve of Destruction" and McGuire loved it. Sloan and Steve Barri taped an instrumental backing for a rough recording of McGuire singing the vocal, which somehow leaked out to a radio station. It was this unfinished mix that was eventually released. It was banned by some radio stations due to its pessimistic message.

McGuire later became a born-again Christian and has sold numerous Christian pop records. "Eve" was hardly Sloan's first or last musical effort. Employed as a songwriter for Trousdale Music, Sloan and Steve Barri provided songs for Jan & Dean, The Rip Chords and their own non-groups like the Fantastic Baggies, The Lifeguards, and Willie and the Wheels.

Grazing in the Grass Hugh Masekela

#1 July 20, 1968 Philemon Hou, Harry Elston

Some years after the 1968 instrumental "Grazing in the Grass" topped the charts, Hugh Masekela referred to it as "very contrived." MCA wanted to use Masekela's South African sound to compete with Herb Alpert's then popular South American sound. The song did well, but Masekela was uncomfortable with altering his style. Hugh Ramapolo Masekela fled his native South Africa in 1960 to attend the Royal Academy of Music in London. He then moved to New York to attend the Manhattan School of Music on a scholarship arranged by Harry Belafonte. Masekela remained exiled from his homeland for thirty years, during which time his unique mix of South African jazz and Western pop and rock brought him success in the West. Through the '70s and '80s Masekela worked in Nigeria, Ghana, Zimbabwe and Botswana, mixing South African jazz with Afro-beat dance rhythms. In 1987 he toured with Paul Simon. Masekela wrote the music to the musical *Sarafina* which was released as the 1992 film *Up Township*. Returning to South Africa in 1990, Masekela began work on his 1993 recording *Hope*, which features his most famous music performed by South African musicians. "Grazing in the Grass" reappeared in 1969, this time with lyrics, in a recording by The Friends of Distinction. In this incarnation it made the top ten on both pop and R & B charts.

Guitar Boogie Shuffle The Virtues

#5 April 27, 1959 Arthur Smith

The Virtues were the brainchild of Frank "Virtue" Virtuoso, a musician from Philadelphia. The group was formed in 1946 after Frank's stint in the Regular Navy Dance Band. They had a boogie sound that drew solid local audiences for many years. In 1958 Virtue wrote an arrangement of a boogie tune written by former Navy buddy Arthur Smith. Adding a shuffle rock beat to it and tossing in a few jazz licks for spice, Virtue basically rewrote the tune. Out of friendship he gave the credit to his old friend. "Guitar Boogie Shuffle" soared to #5 on the charts, selling some two million copies. There was a novelty to the sound of The Virtues' "Shuffle" that apparently wore thin with their follow-up recordings. Although the group broke up in 1962, Frank Virtue kept his hand in the music business, putting together various groups under his name. Virtue also did some successful work as a producer, including "Hey There Lonely Girl" for Eddie Holman.

Happy, Happy Birthday Baby The Tune Weavers

#5 October 28, 1957 Margo Sylvia, Gilbert Lopez

The Tune Weavers' rise to popularity is a tribute to the "I know a guy who knows a guy ..." school of business. Gilbert Lopez sang in an *a cappella* group in his off hours from a Boston-area pattern-making school. His teacher's brother-in-law happened to be Frank Paul, a record label owner and former bandleader. Lopez pestered his teacher, who in turn pestered his brother-in-law and eventually an informal audition was set up. When the group, then known as The Tone Weavers, sang "Happy, Happy Birthday Baby" Frank Paul sat up and took notice. His instincts were good. "Happy, Happy" sold two million copies and sent The Tune Weavers singing across the country. They appeared in Alan Freed's *Rock 'n' Roll Show*, on Dick Clark's *American Bandstand* and at the Apollo Theatre. Despite their national popularity, none of the group's follow-up records caught on. The group, comprised of Johnnie Sylvia, Margo Sylvia, Gilbert Lopez, and Charlotte Davis, eventually split up. Margo Sylvia made a few stabs at a solo career, but the other members left the music business.

Harper Valley P.T.A.   Jeannie C. Riley

#1 September 21, 1968   Tom T. Hall

Jeannie C. Riley (Jeannie Carolyn Stephenson) was a country girl from Anson, Texas, with dreams of country music stardom. She and husband Mickey Riley moved to Nashville and joined the ranks of aspiring musicians working day jobs to get by. Producer Shelby Singleton, Jr. heard a demo of Riley and immediately put her sound together with Tom T. Hall's tune about duplicity in Southern society. Riley's wildest dreams came true. She appeared on *The Ed Sullivan Show* and the TV talk show circuit, bought a purple Cadillac and won the 1968 Grammy for Best Female Country Vocal Performance. "Harper Valley P.T.A." sold some six million copies. Several of Riley's follow-up recordings sold well, but none ever matched the splash made by "Harper Valley." The song inspired a film and a short-lived TV series but these had little effect on Riley. Her career stalled and her marriage ended. Jeannie turned to Gospel music, eventually re-married Mickey, and released "Return to Harper Valley" in 1986.

I Like It Like That   Kris Kenner

#2 July 31, 1961   Kris Kenner, Allen Toussaint

As a performer, Kris Kenner's thoroughly unprofessional demeanor and complete lack of stage presence made him a nightmare to manage. But Kris Kenner the songwriter was another story. Over the years his New Orleans style created hits for Fats Domino, Dave Clark Five, and Wilson Pickett. His own big hit, "I Like It Like That," brought him a Grammy nomination, tours with The Coasters, Gladys Knight & The Pips, and Jackie Wilson, as well as an appearance on *American Bandstand*. The song worked well in various incarnations, with The Bobbettes, Dave Clark Five, and Loggins & Messina all taking renditions of it to the charts. Kenner's days in rock 'n' roll were numbered. After endless struggles with alcoholism he was sent to prison in 1968 for statutory rape, spending four years behind bars. Kenner died of a heart attack in 1976.

Israelites   Desmond Dekker & The Aces

#9 June 28, 1969   Desmond Dekker, Leslie Kong

"Israelites" is one of the best-known reggae songs in the world. Rising to #9 on the U.S. pop charts in 1969, the song sold over one million copies internationally and rose to #1 on the British pop charts. Although Desmond Dekker (born Desmond Dacris) scored several British hits, he never placed on the U.S. charts again. It was reggae musician Bob Marley, who worked with Dekker in a welding shop, that introduced Dekker to Leslie "King" Kong, the co-author of "Israelites." Although a British reissue of "Israelites" landed back in the British Top Ten in 1975, Dekker went for nearly a decade without recording, releasing the album *Black and Dekker* in 1985. He found himself back in the limelight in 1990 when "Israelites" was released yet again following its use on a Maxell Tape commercial in Britain. Dekker won Jamaica's Golden Trophy award five times during the late '60s.

Leader of the Laundromat   The Detergents
#19 January 9, 1965   Paul Vance, Lee Pockriss

"Leader of the Laundromat" was a spoof of The Shangri-Las hit record "Leader of the Pack." Paul Vance, Lee Pockriss, Ron Dante, Danny Jordan and Tommy Wynn got together and made a quick demo of the song. Roulette Records quickly added the name "The Detergents" to the label and it raced up the charts. After the record peaked The Detergents actually materialized as a group and hit the road for a time. Several singles followed "Leader" but none of them rose higher than #89 on the *Billboard* charts. In addition to their fame as The Detergents, the songwriting team of Vance and Pockriss was responsible for such hits as "Catch a

Falling Star," "What Is Love?" and the unforgettable "Itsy Bitsy Teenie Weenie Yellow Polkadot Bikini."

Let Me Go Lover!   Joan Weber
#1 January 1, 1955   Jenny Lou Carson

The story of Joan Weber's career is a classic tale of overnight success. Weber was eighteen years old, married, and expecting her first child when she met up with manager Eddie Joy. Joy introduced her to the producers of CBS's *Studio One*, who were searching for a song to accompany a drama about the dark side of the recording industry. Arnold Shaw, general manager of Hill and Range Songs, took the tune "Let Me Go, Devil!" and rewrote the lyrics omitting all references to liquor. Weber quickly recorded the song with Jimmy Carroll's orchestra. Within a couple of weeks of the song's appearance on *Studio One* it had sold over 500,000 copies. Patti Page, Teresa Brewer, and Sunny Gale recorded their own versions of the song, but

Joan, an unknown, outsold them all. Joan's version of the song sat at #1 on the *Billboard* charts for four weeks. Less than two years after her hit, subsequent appearances on *The Ed Sullivan Show* and with Jack Carter at the Copacabana, the ride was over for Joan. Her record contract was severed and her marriage failed. She continued to perform in Philadelphia bars and worked as a clerk in a New Jersey library. Joan Weber died in 1981.

Love (Can Make You Happy)   Mercy
#2 May 31, 1969   Jack Sigler, Jr.

The group Mercy was born when Tampa high school student Jack Sigler, Jr. picked up a guitar and pulled together a few musical buddies. Mercy was soon seen on stages throughout the Tampa area. Sigler went on to the University of Southern Florida where he managed to keep the band alive. When Hollywood producer George Roberts was on location in Florida he happened to hear the group singing "Love (Can Make You Happy)." He liked what he heard and decided to include them in the film he was making at the time, *Fireball Jungle*. Although the film never saw the light of a projector, the song survived. Eventually Warner Brothers picked it up and sent it on its way to #2. After a couple of luke-warm follow-ups, the group called it quits.

May the Bird of Paradise Fly Up Your Nose   "Little" Jimmy Dickens

#15 December 4, 1965   Neal Merritt

The fact that "May the Bird of Paradise Fly Up Your Nose" made it to #15 on the charts is astounding in its own right. What is truly amazing is that a four-foot-eleven inch country singer in an over-sized Stetson and glittering western wear managed a pop hit nearly a year after The Beatles' first U.S. appearance. Dickens was a familiar name in country and western circles for many years, but "Bird of Paradise" was his first and only score on the pop charts. In 1982 "Little" Jimmy Dickens was voted into the Country Music Hall of Fame.

More   Kai Winding

#8 August 24, 1963   Riz Ortolani, Nino Oliviero, M. Ciorciolini

Danish-born Kai Winding was twelve years old when his family came to the United States. Like many U.S. teens, Kai joined the high school band where he learned to play the trombone. He was only eighteen when he hooked up with Shorty Allen's band. Winding went on to become a major presence on the Big Band circuit, recording with the likes of Benny Goodman and Stan Kenton. He played New York jazz clubs during the '50s, winning the job of music director at the New York City Playboy Club in 1962. He experimented with combinations of electronic and acoustic instruments and in 1963 recorded his one pop hit "More." Winding eventually made his way to Los Angeles where he became one of the top studio trombonists of his generation. Kai Winding died in 1983.

More Today than Yesterday   Spiral Starecase

#12 June 14, 1969   Pat Upton

"More Today than Yesterday" was the second single cut by the Sacramento-based group Spiral Starecase. After playing the lesser clubs of the Sacramento and Reno areas for five years, group members Pat Upton, Harvey Kaye, Dick Lopes, Vinny Parello, and Bobby Raymond were more than ready for a break. To give their single an edge in the marketplace the group augmented their sound by bringing in brass players. After the single took off, the group released two follow-up records that placed low on the charts. The brassy sound that brought the group its success also caused its downfall. Unable to reproduce their slick, studio sound in concert, the group was a disappointment to live audiences.

Na Na Hey Hey Kiss Him Goodbye   Steam
#1 December 6, 1969   Gary DeCarlo, Paul Leka, Dale Frashuer

The group Steam didn't exist until their #1 hit "Na Na Hey Hey Kiss Him Goodbye" demanded a follow-up tour. The song, now the theme-song for the Chicago White Sox, was written on demand for the B-side of a Gary DeCarlo solo recording. Songwriters DeCarlo, Paul Leka and Dale Frashuer pulled out a folksy ballad from their days as members of the Chateaus. Their intent was to rework it and use it as the throw-away B-side tune they needed. Despite the songwriters' embarrassment over the slapped-together song, Mercury Records loved and released it as an A-side single. None of the three wanted their name attached to the song so they invented the name Steam. After a follow-up tour by musicians from Bridgeport, Connecticut, working under the name Steam, another album was needed. DeCarlo decided to call a halt to the charade and refused to write any more songs for the "group."

On Top of Spaghetti   Tom Glazer & The Do-Re-Mi Children's Chorus
#14 July 6, 1963   Tom Glazer

Tom Glazer's one hit record was a parody on Burl Ives' recording of the folk classic "On Top of Old Smokey." Although his pop star days were few, he maintained a long and interesting performing career. Glazer was born in 1914 in Philadelphia. After several years of playing in jazz groups and military bands, Glazer turned to performing folk music - mostly for children. During the forties he was frequently heard on the radio in such shows as *Listening Post, Theatre Guild on the Air, True Story, We the People,* and his own ABC radio show *Tom Glazer's Music Box*. During the '50s and '60s he performed folk music, cutting successful records on the Young People's label. Glazer was well-known in musical circles as a songwriter and lyricist. His credits include "Melody of Love," "More," "Old Soldiers Never Die," "Pussy Cat," "Skokiaan," and "Till We Two Are One."

Pipeline   The Chantays
#4 May 4, 1963   Bob Spickard, Brian Carman

"Pipeline," one of the best known songs of the surfing genre, started out as "Liberty's Whip," was changed to "44 Magnum," and eventually took its name from the legendary Hawaiian Pipeline. In the end it became a #4 hit for The Chantays, a group made up of songwriters Bob Spickard and Brian Carman with buddies Warren Walters, Bob Marshall and Bob Welch. All five were still enrolled in high school when "Pipeline" was released. Despite the success of the song, the group itself was not destined to succeed. Since The Chantays had high school classes to attend, a follow-up tour was impossible. An album followed, complete with a few cuts pulled out as singles, but the group went nowhere. The Chantays spent the summer of 1964 touring Hawaii before they broke up. Spickard, Carman and Welch all maintain day jobs and play together in the Catalina Good Time Band. Marshall still performs in a country and western band during his off hours from a teaching career.

Pretty Little Angel Eyes   Curtis Lee
#7 August 7, 1961   Tommy Boyce, Curtis Lee

A good deal of the credit for Curtis Lee's success with "Pretty Little Angel Eyes" must go to record producer Phil Spector. Spector, who began as a member of The Teddy Bears and later created the Wall of Sound rock phenomenon, gave Curtis Lee the polished sound that made the song a hit. With background doo-wops provided by The Halos the record quickly hit #7. Lee's "Under the Moon," also produced by Spector, made it to #46 on the charts that same year. Spector left Dunes Records and Lee tried for continued success with several more recordings. Without the assistance of the Spector touch, Lee's uneven voice was never to bring him another hit.

Sea of Love   Phil Phillips with The Twilights
#2 August 24, 1959   George Khoury, Phil Baptiste

Had the gas company meter-reader not heard John Phillip Baptiste practicing a love song he had written, "Sea of Love" would never have hit the nation's airwaves. The meter-reader knew about record producer George Khoury and suggested that Baptiste, who was a bell-hop at the time, get in touch with him. Khoury liked the song. He talked John into changing his name and pulled in a group called the Cupcakes to provide instrumentals for Baptiste and his background singers. In short order Khoury found himself leasing the song to Mercury for independent distribution. After turning out several more singles, none of which scored, Baptiste became a D.J. in Louisiana. He produced a cover of "Sea of Love" recorded by the Fire Ants, a group made up of five of his children. Del Shannon made it to #33 on the charts with "Sea" in 1982 and The Honeydrippers (Robert Plant, Jimmy Page, Jeff Beck and Nile Rodgers) hit #3 with another version of it in 1984.

Silhouettes   The Rays
#3 November 4, 1957   Frank C. Slay Jr., Bob Crewe

Songwriter Bob Crewe was riding a train in Philadelphia one evening when he spotted the silhouette of an embracing couple. The image was memorable enough for him to mention it to his friend Frank Slay, who also happened to be his songwriting partner and fellow founder of XYZ Records. Slay thought there was a song in it somewhere and wrote a plot line. Crewe added a chorus and the two realized they had a decent song on their hands. Slay was working a day job at Cameo Records at the time, where he heard the audition of a group called The Rays. The Rays were not quite what Cameo was hoping to find. Slay and Crewe put The Rays together with "Silhouettes" and added a B-side of "Daddy Cool," creating hits with both tunes. The Rays managed to get back onto the charts a few times over the coming years but never managed another hit.

Stay   Maurice Williams & The Zodiacs
#1 November 21, 1960   Maurice Williams

By the time Maurice Williams & The Zodiacs finally got an acceptable cut of "Stay" they were fairly sick of the little tune. Destined to be the shortest #1 hit in pop music history, "Stay" also proved to have a staying power no one could have imagined. The tune also became a hit for The Hollies in 1963, The Four Seasons in 1964, Rufus & Chaka Khan in 1978, and Jackson Browne in 1978. The Zodiacs never scored another big hit, although the group remained a solid entity on the "beach music" scene for many years. They maintained a steady local following in the Southeast and toured with Chuck Berry and James Brown during the '60s. Maurice Williams got the pop music bug in high school, forming a group called the Royal Charmers with a few buddies. Taking the name The Gladiolas, the group added a couple of members and cut a few records, including a now nearly forgotten version of "Little Darlin'." Reorganizing and picking up the name The Zodiacs from a foreign car, the group had one more false start. In 1960 Williams put together an ensemble that clicked, and re-used the Zodiac name. The new group included Wiley Bennett, Henry Gaston (Gaston sings the falsetto break on the recording), Albert Hill, Little Willie Morrow, and Charles Thomas. The Zodiacs were inducted into the Beach Music Hall of Fame in 1985.

Stranger on the Shore   Mr. Acker Bilk
#1 May 26, 1962   Acker Bilk, Robert Mellin

Nothing about the success of "Stranger on the Shore" made much sense. A sedate instrumental, the record spent over a year on the British pop charts, selling over four million copies. While jazz clarinetist Acker Bilk had little in common with The Beatles, his recording was the first British act to hit number one on the American pop charts, a spot The Beatles were soon to know well. Although Bilk and his oh-so-British bowler hat were soon eclipsed by the long-haired kids of the British Invasion, he maintained a successful musical career in Britain. Acker's jazz career began in the '50s. He formed a band of his own by mid-decade that had a Dixie/shuffle sound featuring frequent clarinet solos. Acker stayed with traditional jazz, leading several noteworthy British bands for over thirty years. Bilk appeared in two Royal Command Performances and became a radio personality via *Acker's 'Alf 'Our* on the BBC.

Sukiyaki   Kyu Sakamoto
#1 June 15, 1963   Hachidai Nakamura, Rokusuke Ei

Kyu Sakamoto had one hit in the U.S., a sob-story titled "Sukiyaki." Sakamoto has the distinction of being one of only three Japanese artists ever to score on the *Billboard Hot 100* chart, and the only one to do so with a song sung completely in Japanese. By the time "Sukiyaki" hit the states, Sakamoto had already managed over a dozen hits in Japan and had appeared in ten films as well as on radio and TV.

"Sukiyaki" was titled "Ue O Muite Aruko" ("I Look Up When I Walk") in Japanese. The phrase comes from the lyrics "... I look up when I walk so the tears won't fall." Kyu Sakamoto died on August 12, 1985, one of the 520 passengers lost in the crash of Japan Airlines 747 outside Tokyo.

Tie Me Kangaroo Down Sport   Rolf Harris

#3 July 13, 1963   Rolf Harris

The curious tune "Tie Me Kangaroo Down, Sport" may be familiar to Americans from its many months of airplay, but the name of Rolf Harris, its Australian composer and performer, has largely been forgotten. Not so in Australia and Britain, where "Tie Me Kangaroo" was a hit three years before it charted in the U.S. Harris, who worked as a TV cartoonist in London, had several hits on both the British and Australian charts. He had two television series and twice won medals from the Order of the British Empire. In this country however, it is his quirky tune and his "wobbling" that brought him a brief taste of fame. Wobbling, for the uninitiated, consists of shaking a warped piece of Masonite, using its strange sounds as percussion effects. When "Tie Me Kangaroo Down Sport" was at the height of its popularity in Britain, warped pieces of Masonite were all the rage, with over 50,000 pieces sold to consumers for use as "musical instruments."

Who Put the Bomp
(In the Bomp Ba Bomp Ba Bomp)   Barry Mann

#7 September 25, 1961   Barry Mann, Gerry Goffin

Barry Mann the performer may have scored only one big hit, but Barry Mann the songwriter has several decades of hits to his credit. "Somewhere Out There," which he wrote with his wife, songwriter Cynthia Weil, won a Grammy in 1986. The pair also produced "You've Lost that Lovin' Feeling," "I Love How You Love Me" and "Blame It on the Bossa Nova," to mention a few. Although he started with ukulele lessons in Brooklyn as a child, Barry Mann has often claimed that he can hardly read or write music. In 1961 Mann was persuaded to record a few of his own songs. His third record, the novelty song "Who Put the Bomp (In the Bomp Ba Bomp Ba Bomp)" was his only real success. He said later that it was just a take-off on doo-wop recordings.

The Worst That Could Happen   Brooklyn Bridge

#3 February 1, 1969   Jim Webb

Scoring a hit record in 1969 was old news for Johnny Maestro (John Maestrangelo). Maestro had been a member of The Crests during 1959 and '60 when they charted with "Sixteen Candles," "The Angels Listened In," "Step by Step," and "Trouble in Paradise." After some success on his own Maestro tried to resurrect The Crests. Failing at that, he joined the Del Satins. At a Battle of the Bands competition on Long Island, Maestro and his group bumped into a band called the Rhythm Method. The two bands decided to join forces, at which point someone said of the new, eleven-member band: "That is going to be as easy to sell as the Brooklyn Bridge." Hence the name. By the time Brooklyn Bridge cut its second single, a cover of the Fifth Dimension's "The Worst That Could Happen," they had hit their stride and the single shot up the charts. It was a never-to-be-repeated success, however. In the early '70s Brooklyn Bridge shortened their name to Bridge. Reduced in number to five members, Bridge performed as a pop-rock band throughout the '80s. As of the mid-'90s, Maestro and the group were still performing.

Alley Cat Song

Words by JACK HARLEN
Music by FRANK BJORN

He goes on the prowl each night like an al-ley cat,

look-in' for some new de-light like an al-ley cat.

She can't trust him out of sight, there's no doubt of that.
He don't know what "faith-ful" means, there's no doubt of that.

Angel of the Morning

Words and Music by
CHIP TAYLOR

There'll be no strings to bind _ your hands, ___ not if my love can't bind your
May - be the sun's light will _ be dim, ___ and it won't mat - ter an - y -

heart;
how;

and there's no need to take a
if morn-ing's ech - o says we've

stand _ for it was I who chose to start.
sinned, _ well, it was what I want-ed now.

Apache

By JERRY LORDAN

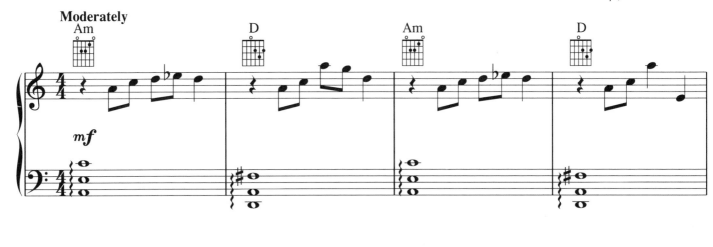

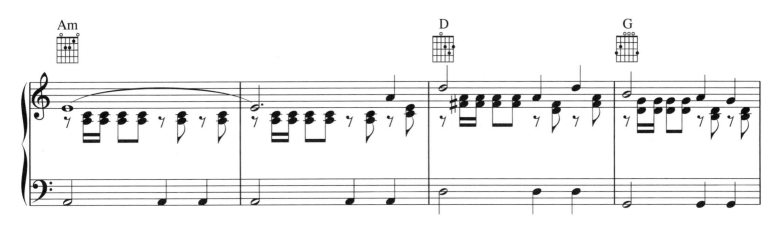

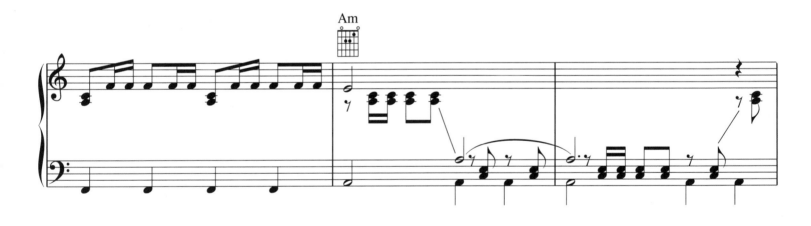

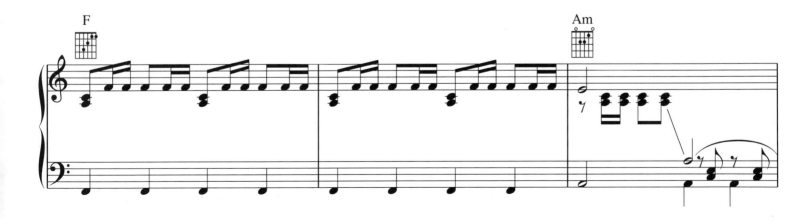

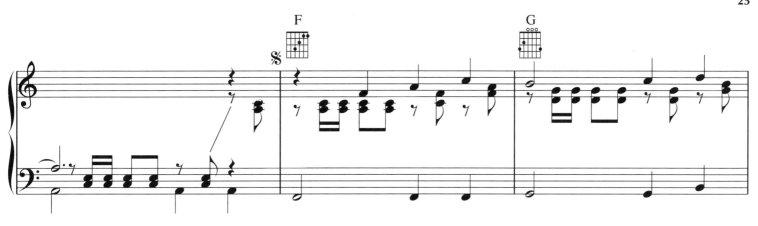

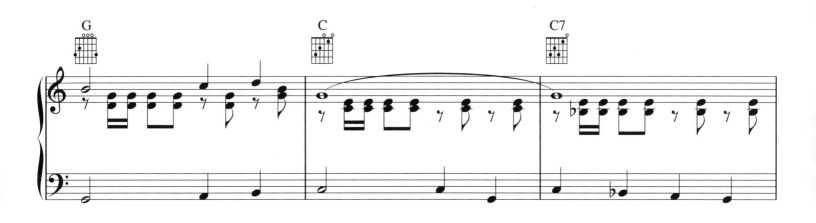

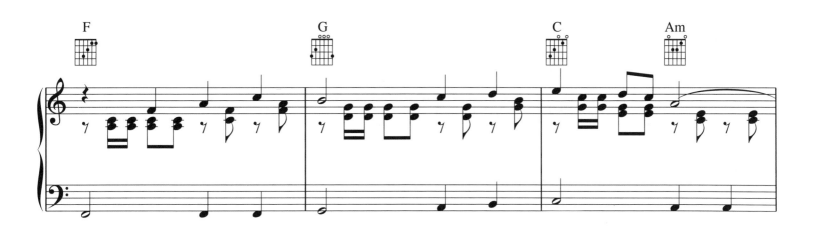

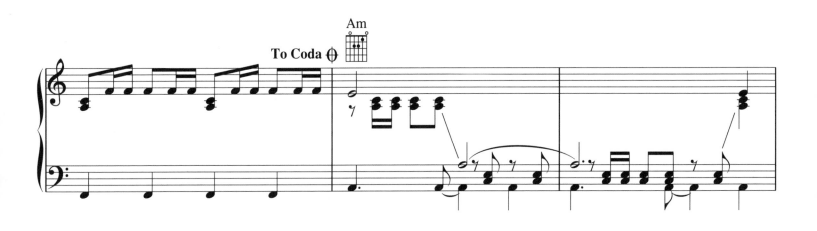

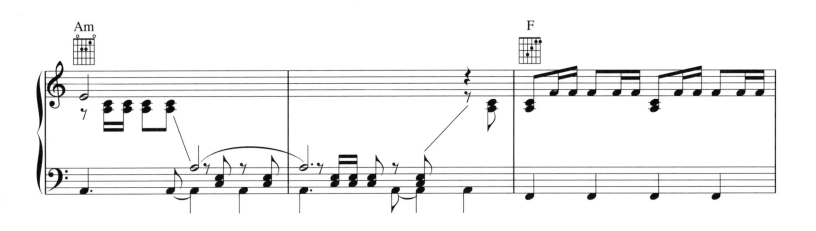

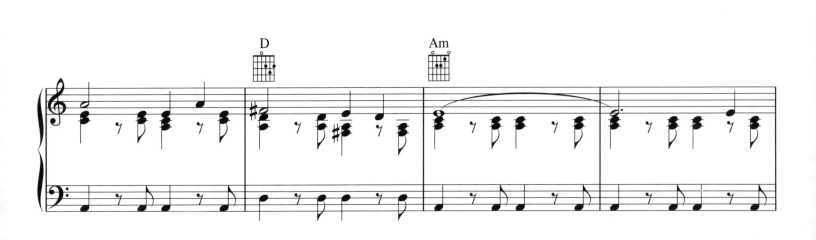

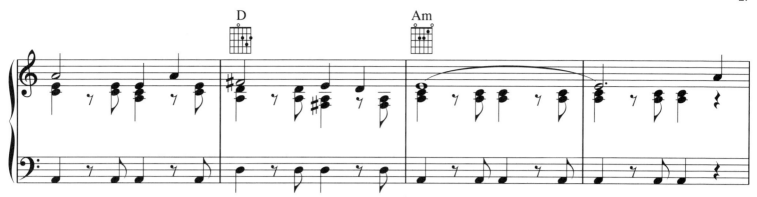

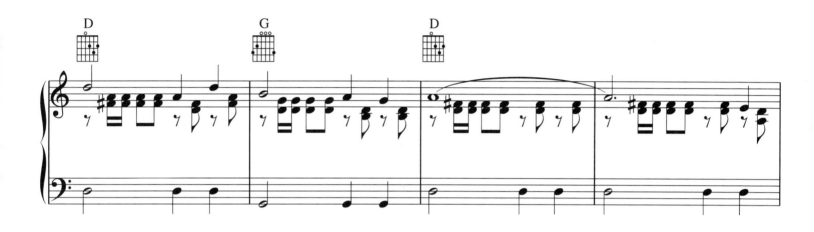

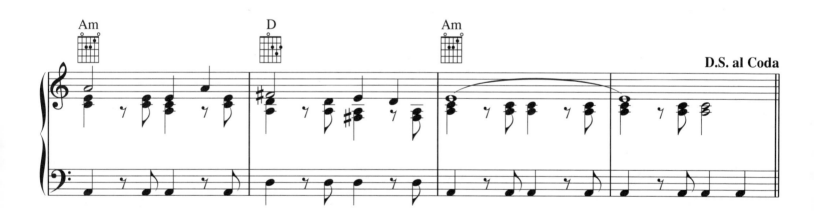

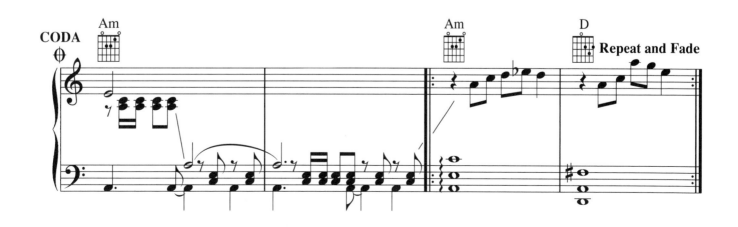

Theme from
"Baby, the Rain Must Fall"

Words and Music by ELMER BERNSTEIN
and ERNIE SHELDON

Some men climb a moun-tain. Some men swim the sea. My
do not love for sil - ver. Do not swim love for gold. I
am not rich or fa - mous, but who can ev - er tell.

Some men fly a - bove the sky. They are what they must be.
heart is mine to give a - way. It nev - er will be sold.
do not know what waits for me, may-be heav - en may be hell.

The Birds and the Bees

Words and Music by
HERB NEWMAN

Let me tell ya 'bout the birds and the bees and the flow-ers and the trees and the

moon up a-bove and a thing called love

Let me tell ya 'bout the stars in the sky and a girl and a guy and the

facts of life___ start-ing from "A" to "Z". Let me tell ya 'bout the

birds and the bees and the flow-ers and the trees and the moon up a-bove

and a thing___ called love.___

Let me tell ya 'bout the love.___

Bobby's Girl

Words and Music by GARY KLEIN
and HENRY HOFFMAN

That's the most __ im - por - tant thing __ to me. _____

no chord

_____ And if __ I was _____ Bob - by's girl; __ if __ I was __

__ Bob - by's girl, __ what a faith - ful,

thank - ful girl I'd be. _____

1

2

Book of Love

Words and Music by WARREN DAVIS,
GEORGE MALONE and CHARLES PATRICK

Tell me, tell me, tell me, Oh, who wrote the book of love? I've

got to know the an-swer, Was it some-one from a-bove? I won-der, won-der

who, _____ who, who wrote the book of love? _____

Chantilly Lace

Moderate Boogie Woogie

Words and Music by
J.P. RICHARDSON

Guitar Boogie Shuffle

By ARTHUR SMITH

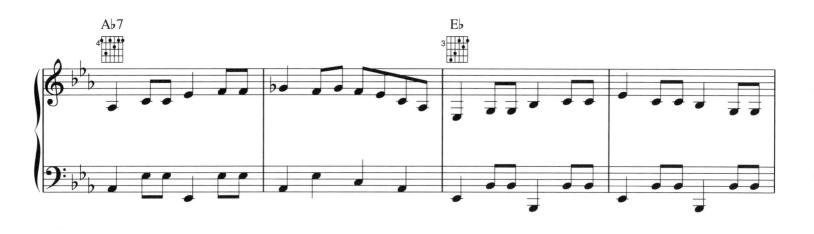

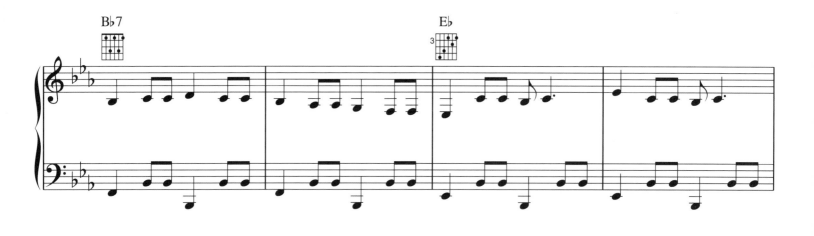

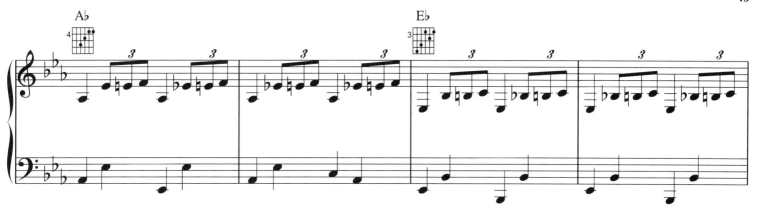

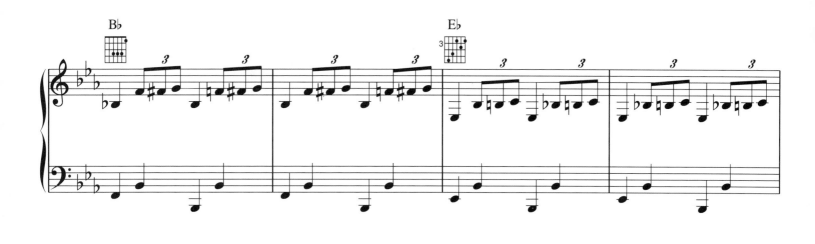

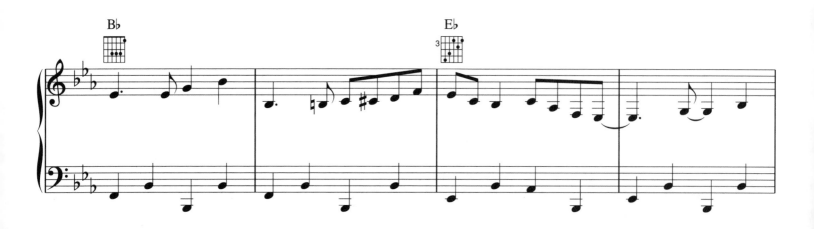

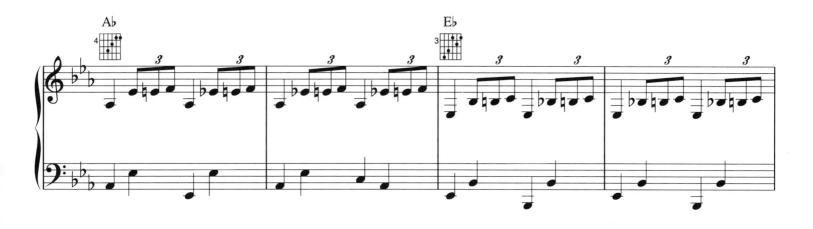

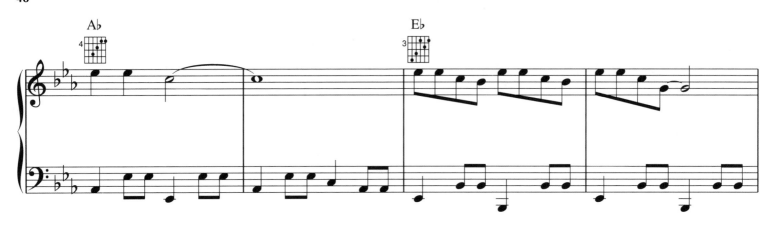

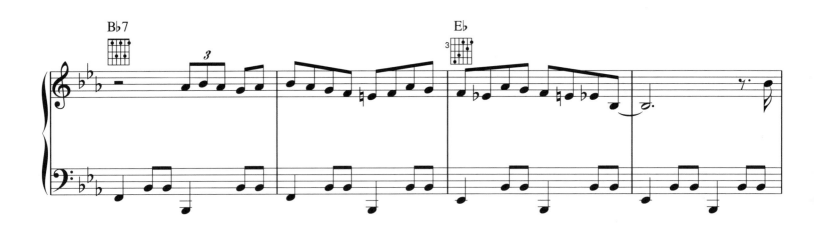

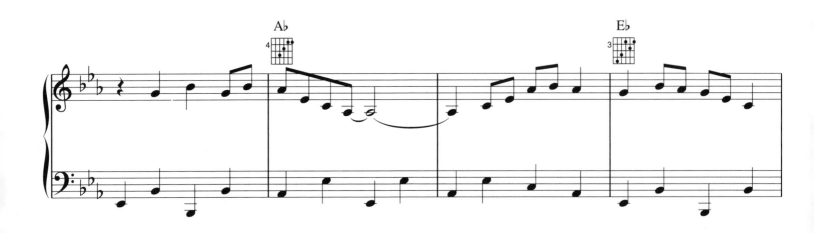

Dominique
from THE SINGING NUN

English Lyrics and Arrangement by NOEL REGNEY
By SOEUR SOURIRE

Bright and lilty

CHORUS

(English) Do - mi - ni - que, nique, nique, o - ver the
(French) Do - mi - ni - que, ni - que, ni - que S'en al

land he plods a - long, And sings a lit - tle
lait tout sim - ple - ment, Rou - tier pau - vreet chan -

song;_____ nev - er ask - ing for re - ward, He just
tant_____ En - tous che - mins, en - tous lieux, Il ne

talks a - bout the Lord, He just talks a - bout the Lord.
parle que du bon Dieu, Il ne parle que du bon Dieu._____

To Coda

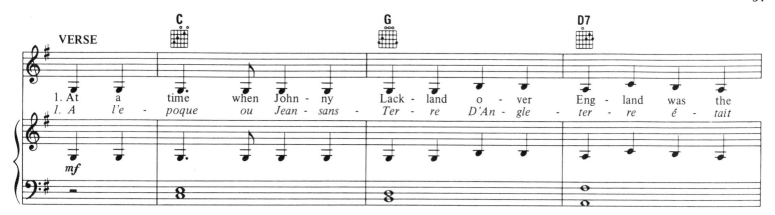

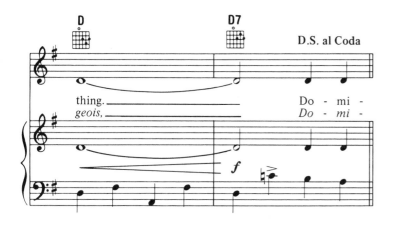

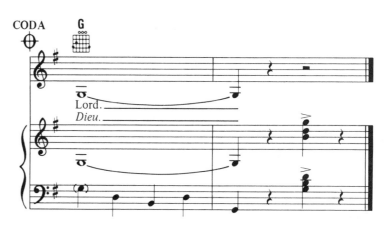

ENGLISH	FRENCH
2. Now a herectic, one day, Among the thorns forced him to crawl. Dominique with just one prayer, Made him hear the good Lord call. (To Chorus)	*2. Certain jour un hérétique Par des ronces le conduit Mais notre Père Dominique Par sa joie le convertit. (Au refrain)*
3. Without horse or fancy wagon, He crossed Europe up and down. Poverty was his companion, As he walked from town to town. (To Chorus)	*3. Ni chameau, ni diligence Il parcourt l'Europe à pied. Scandinavie ou Provence Dans la sainte pauvreté. (Au refrain)*
4. To bring back the straying liars And the lost sheep to the fold, He brought forth the Preaching Friars, Heaven's soldiers, brave and bold. (To Chorus)	*4. Enflamma de toute école Filles et garçons pleins d'ardeur, Et pour semer la Parole Inventa les Frères-Prêcheurs. (Au refrain)*
5. One day, in the budding Order, There was nothing left to eat. Suddenly two angels walked in With a load of bread and meat. (To Chorus)	*5. Chez Dominique et ses frères Le pain s'en vint à manquer Et deux anges se présentèrent Portant de grands pains dorés. (Au refrain)*
6. Dominique once, in his slumber, Saw the Virgin's coat unfurled Over Friars without number Preaching all around the world. (To Chorus)	*6. Dominique vit en rêve Les prêcheurs du monde entier Sous le manteau de la Vierge En grand nombre rassemblés. (Au refrain)*
7. Grant us now, oh Dominique, The grace of love and simple mirth, That we all may help to quicken Godly life and truth on earth. (To Chorus)	*7. Dominique, mon bon Père, Garde-nous simples et gais Pour annoncer à nos frères La Vie et la Vérité. (Au refrain)*

Eve of Destruction

Words and Music by
P.F. SLOAN

Additional Lyrics

3. My blood's so mad feels like coagulatin'
   I'm sittin' here just contemplatin'
   You can't twist the truth it knows no regulatin'
   And a handful of Senators don't pass legislation
   Marches alone can't bring integration
   When human respect is disintegratin'
   This whole crazy world is just too frustatin'.
   (To Chorus:)

4. Think of all the hate there is in Red China
   Then take a look around to Selma, Alabama!
   You may leave here for four days in space
   But when you return, it's the same old place,
   The pounding drums, the pride and disgrace
   You can bury your dead, but don't leave a trace
   Hate your next door neighbor, but don't forget to say grace.
   (To Chorus:)

Grazing in the Grass

Words by HARRY ELSTON
Music by PHILEMON HOU

58

The Deck of Cards

Words and Music by
T. TEXAS TYLER

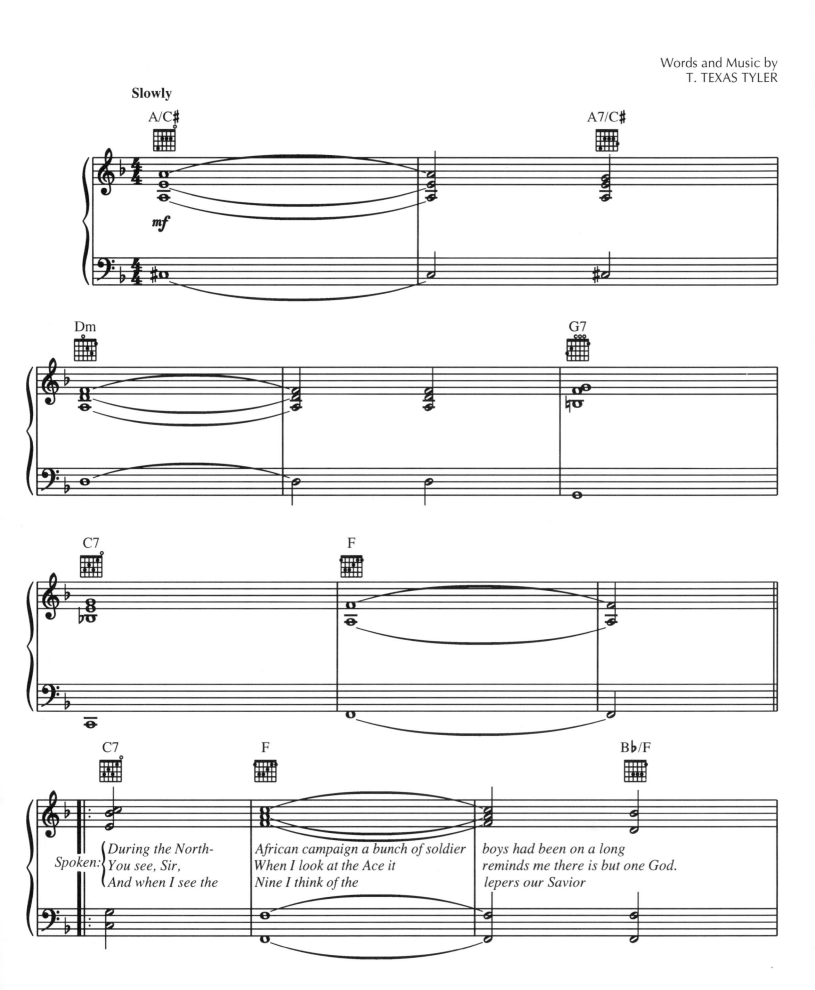

Spoken: { During the North-
You see, Sir,
And when I see the

African campaign a bunch of soldier
When I look at the Ace it
Nine I think of the

boys had been on a long
reminds me there is but one God.
lepers our Savior

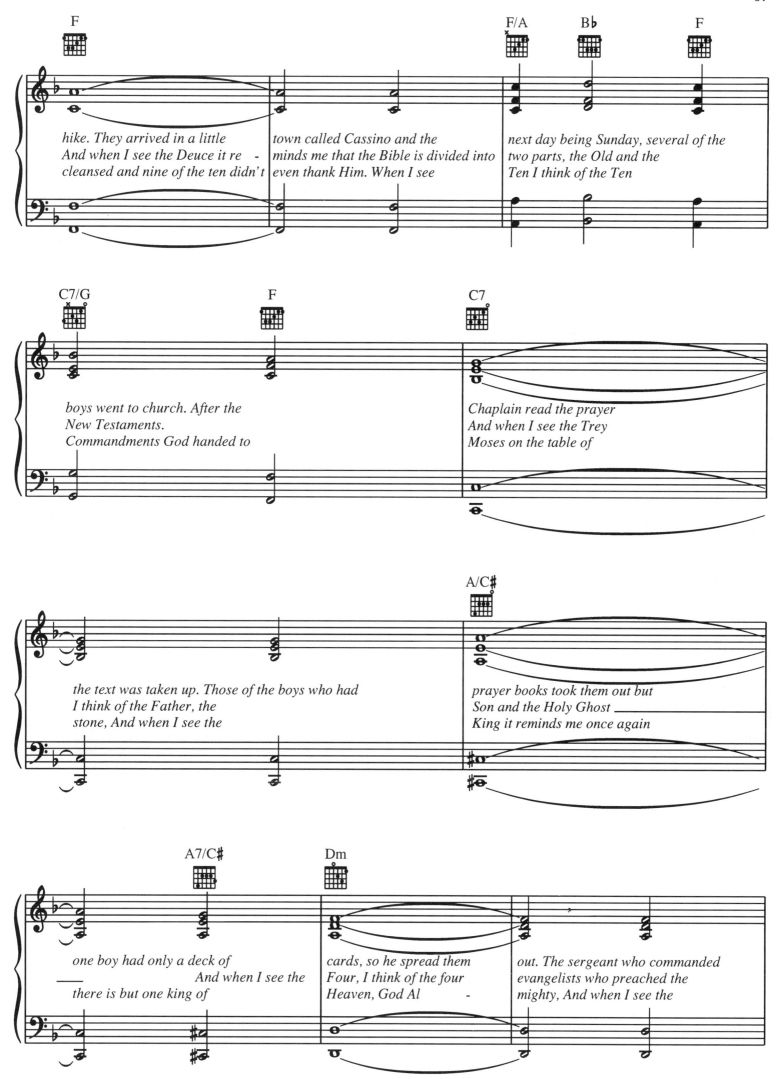

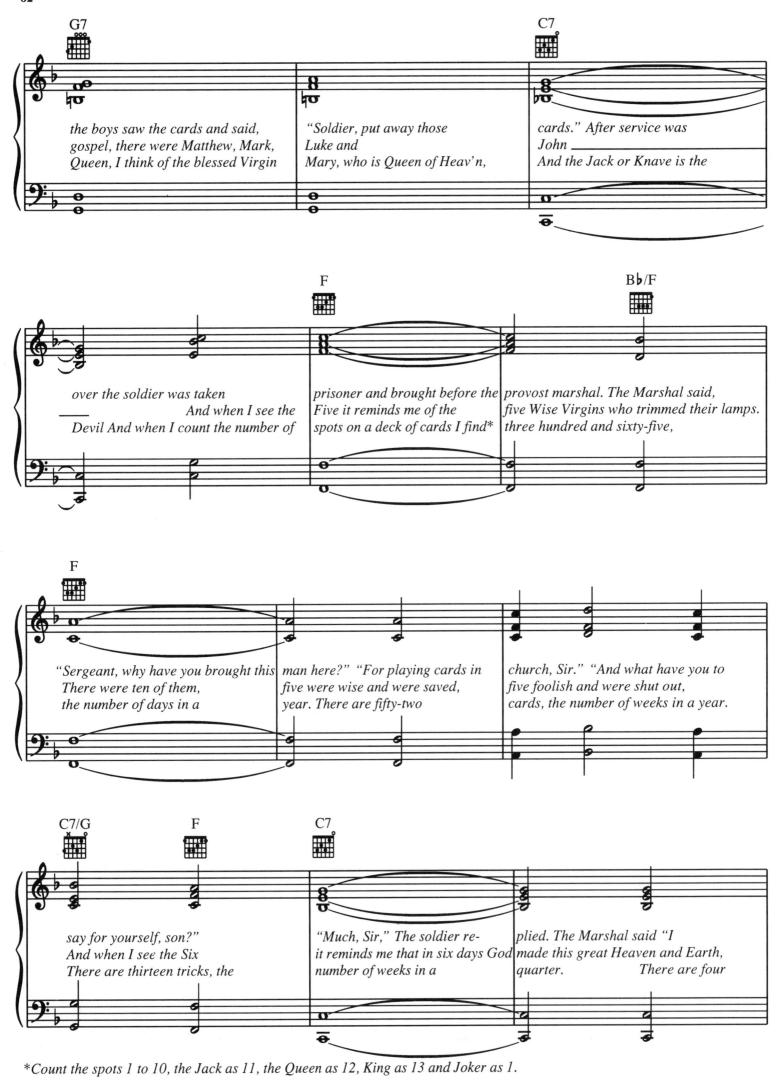

G7

the boys saw the cards and said,
gospel, there were Matthew, Mark,
Queen, I think of the blessed Virgin

"Soldier, put away those
Luke and
Mary, who is Queen of Heav'n,

C7

cards." After service was
John _____
And the Jack or Knave is the

F

over the soldier was taken
_____ And when I see the
Devil And when I count the number of

prisoner and brought before the
Five it reminds me of the
spots on a deck of cards I find*

Bb/F

provost marshal. The Marshal said,
five Wise Virgins who trimmed their lamps.
three hundred and sixty-five,

F

"Sergeant, why have you brought this
There were ten of them,
the number of days in a

man here?" "For playing cards in
five were wise and were saved,
year. There are fifty-two

church, Sir." "And what have you to
five foolish and were shut out,
cards, the number of weeks in a year.

C7/G   **F**   **C7**

say for yourself, son?"
And when I see the Six
There are thirteen tricks, the

"Much, Sir," The soldier re-
it reminds me that in six days God
number of weeks in a

plied. The Marshal said "I
made this great Heaven and Earth,
quarter.   There are four

*Count the spots 1 to 10, the Jack as 11, the Queen as 12, King as 13 and Joker as 1.

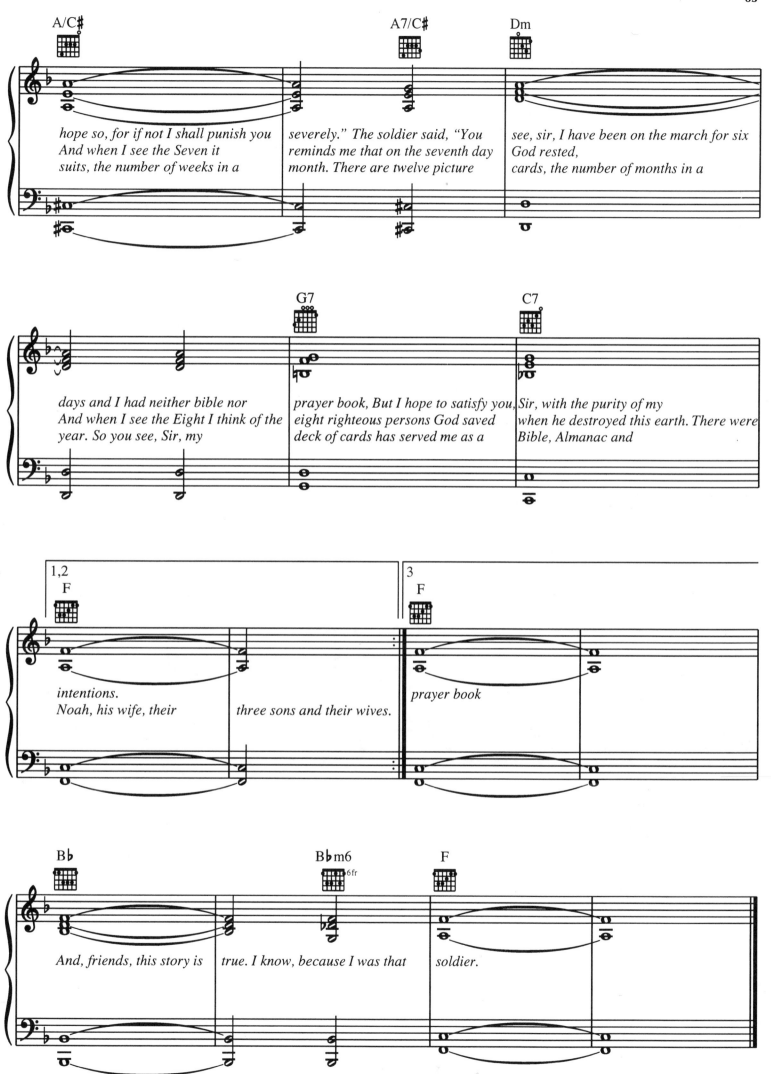

Happy, Happy Birthday Baby

Words and Music by MARGO SYLVIA
and GILBERT LOPEZ

I Like It Like That

Words and Music by KRIS KENNER
and ALLEN TOUSSAINT

Harper Valley P.T.A.

Words and Music by
TOM T. HALL

Moderately (with a heavy beat)

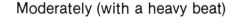

I want to tell you all a stor-y 'bout a Har-per Val-ley wid-owed wife
note said, "Mis-ses John-son, you're wear-ing your dres-ses way too high;
hap-pened that the P. T. A. was gon-na meet that ver-y af-ter-noon;

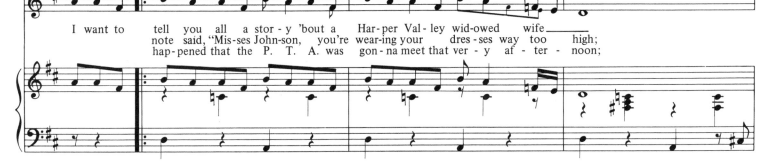

Who had a teen-age daugh-ter who at-tend-ed, Har-per Val-ley Jun-ior
It's re-port-ed you've been drink-ing and a run-nin' 'round with men and go-ing
They were sure sur-prised when Mis-ses John-son wore her mi-ni-skirt in-to the

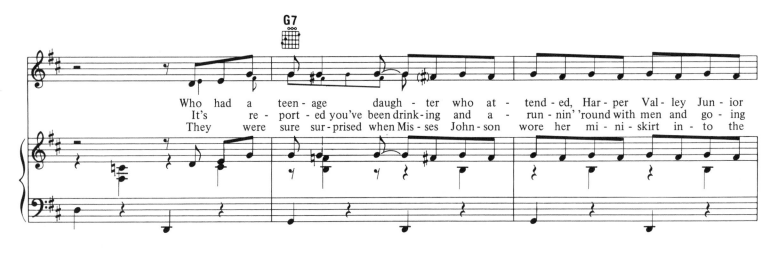

high.
wild: Well her daugh-ter came home one af-ter-
room.   And we don't be-lieve you ought to be a-
          And as she walked up to the black-board, I

Israelites

Words and Music by DESMOND DEKKER
and LESLIE KONG

Additional Lyrics

2. My wife and my kids, they pack up and leave me;
   "Darling," she said, "I'm yours to receive."
   Poor me, the Israelite. Aah!

3. Shirt them ah tear up, trousers are gone;
   I don't want to end up like Bonnie and Clyde.
   Poor me, the Israelite. Aah!

4. After a storm there must be a calm,
   They catch me in the farm, you sound the alarm.
   Poor me, the Israelite. Aah!

Leader of the Laundromat

Words and Music by PAUL VANCE
and LEE POCKRISS

fin - 'lly dry. _____ But I won't for - get your love, ___ oh, lead - er of the

laun - dro - mat. _

Oo, _____

oo. _____

(Spoken:) Who's that bangin' on the piano? I dunno.

Let Me Go Lover!

Words and Music by
JENNY LOU CARSON

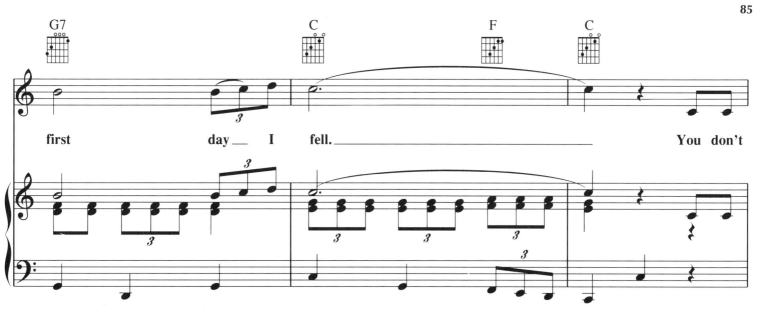

first day__ I fell._____ You don't

want me but you want me to go on __ want - ing

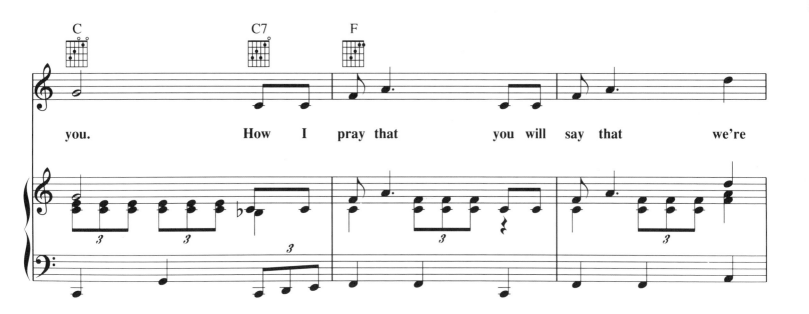

you. How I pray that you will say that we're

through. _____ Please turn me loose, __ what's the

use, __ let __ me go, lov - er. Let me

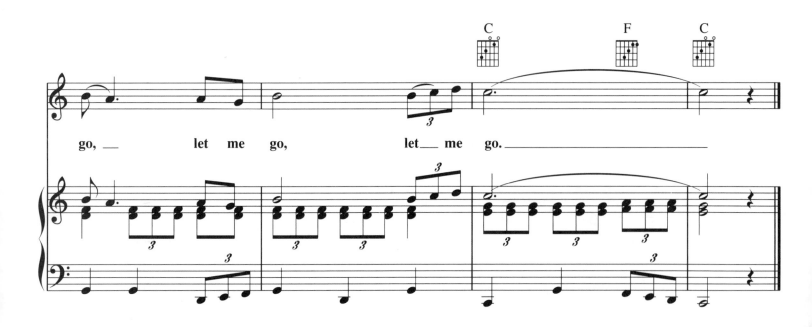

go, __ let me go, let __ me go. _____

Love
(Can Make You Happy)

Words and Music by
JACK SIGLER, JR.

May the Bird of Paradise
Fly Up Your Nose

Words and Music by
NEAL MERRITT

More
(Ti Guardero' Nel Cuore)
from the film MONDO CANE

Music by NINO OLIVIERO and RIZ ORTOLANI
Italian Lyrics by MARCELLO CIORCIOLINI
English Lyrics by NORMAN NEWELL

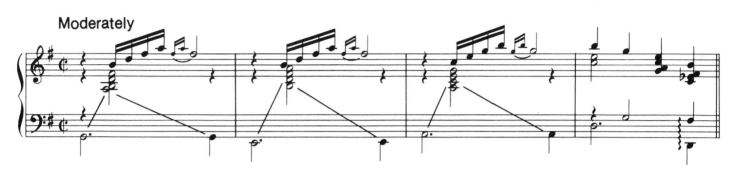

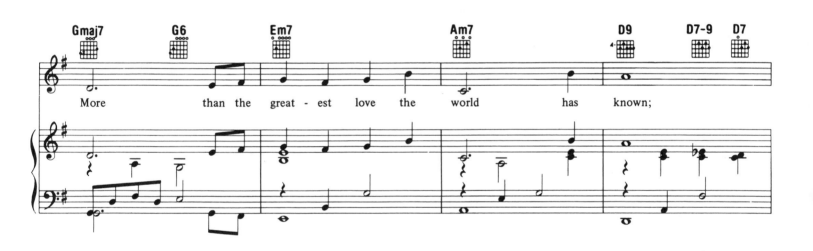

More than the great-est love the world has known;

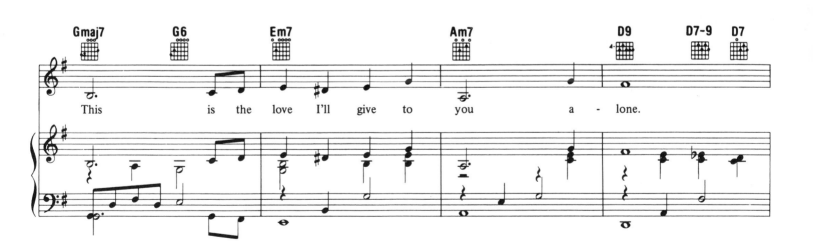

This is the love I'll give to you a - lone.

More Today than Yesterday

Words and Music by
PAT UPTON

Na Na Hey Hey Kiss Him Goodbye

Words and Music by GARY DeCARLO,
PAUL LEKA and DALE FRASHUER

On Top of Spaghetti

Words and Music by
TOM GLAZER

Pipeline

Words and Music by BOB SPICKARD
and BRIAN CARMAN

Pretty Little Angel Eyes

Words and Music by TOMMY BOYCE
and CURTIS LEE

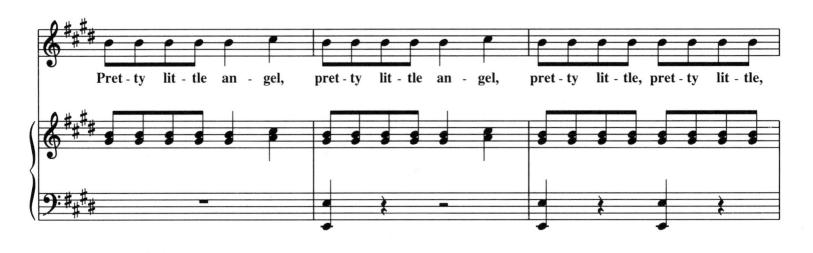

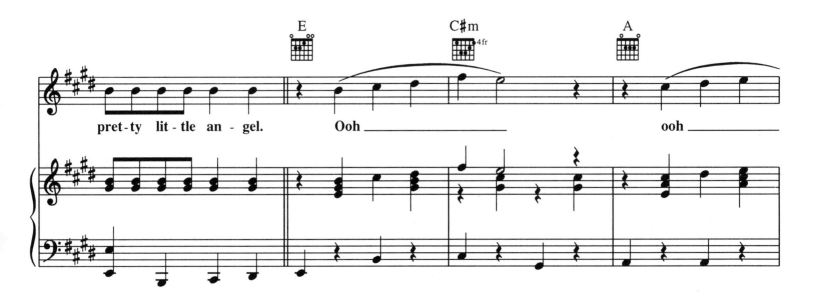

Sea of Love

Words and Music by GEORGE KHOURY
and PHILIP BAPTISTE

Medium Slow Fifties Rock

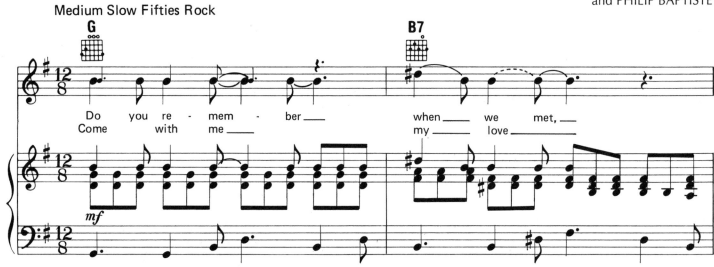

Do you re-mem-ber ____ when ____ we met, ____
Come with me ____ my ____ love ____

that's the day ____ I knew you were my pet.
to the sea, ____ the sea ____ of love.

I ____ want to tell you

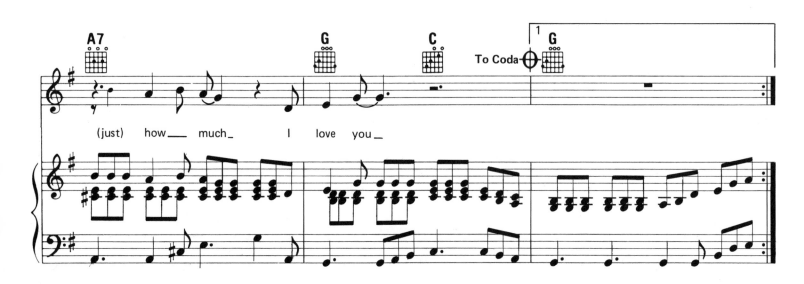

(just) how ____ much ____ I love you ____

To Coda

112

Stranger on the Shore

Words by ROBERT MELLIN
Music by ACKER BILK

Silhouettes

Words and Music by FRANK C. SLAY JR.
and BOB CREWE

Stay

Words and Music by
MAURICE WILLIAMS

Moderately

Sukiyaki

Words and Music by HACHIDAI NAKAMURA and ROKUSUKE EI
English Lyrics by TOM LESLIE and BUZZ CASON

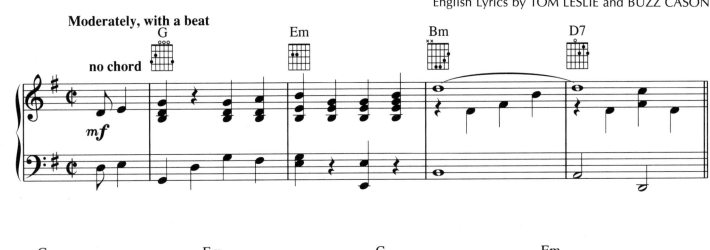

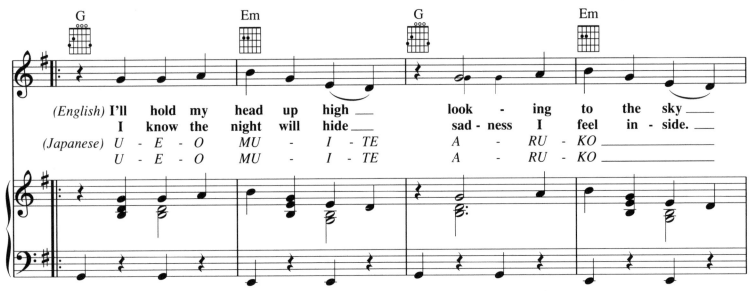

(English) I'll hold my head up high ___ look - ing to the sky ___
I know the night will hide ___ sad - ness I feel in - side.
(Japanese) U - E - O MU - I - TE A - RU - KO ___
U - E - O MU - I - TE A - RU - KO ___

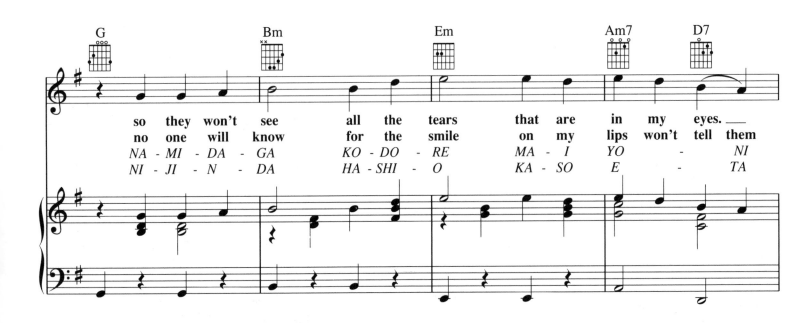

so they won't see all the tears that are in my eyes. ___
no one will know for the smile on my lips won't tell them
NA - MI - DA - GA KO - DO - RE MA - I YO - NI
NI - JI - N - DA HA - SHI - O KA - SO E - TA

124

Who Put the Bomp
(In the Bomp Ba Bomp Ba Bomp)

Words and Music by BARRY MANN
and GERRY GOFFIN

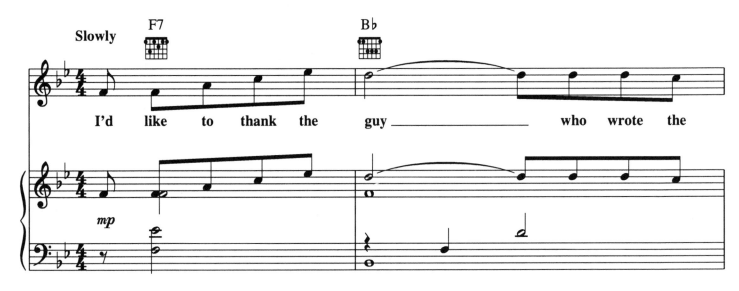

I'd like to thank the guy _____ who wrote the

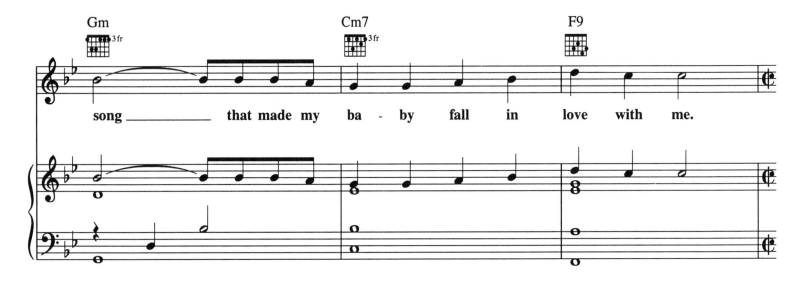

song _____ that made my ba - by fall in love with me.

With a beat

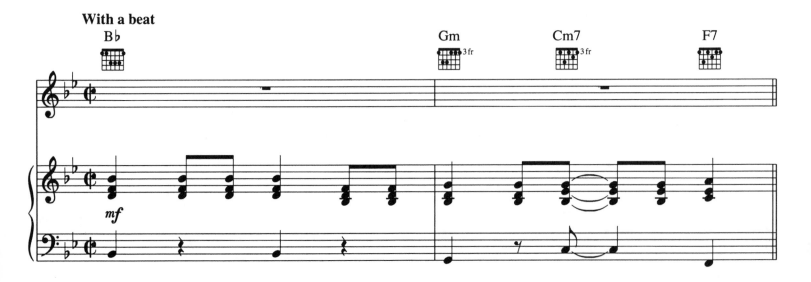

The Worst That Could Happen

Words and Music by
JIM WEBB

Tie Me Kangaroo Down Sport

Words and Music by
ROLF HARRIS

135

Additional lyrics

2. Keep me cockatoo cool, Curl,
   Keep me cockatoo cool.
   Don't go acting the fool, Curl,
   Just keep me cockatoo cool...
   All together now!
   Chorus

3. Take me koala back, Jack,
   Take me koala back.
   He lives somewhere out on the track, Mac,
   So take me koala back.
   All together now!
   Chorus

4. Let me abos go loose, Lew,
   Let me abos go loose.
   They're of no further use, Lew,
   So let me abos go loose.
   All together now!
   Chorus

5. Mind me platypus duck, Bill,
   Mind me platypus duck.
   Don't let him go running amok, Bill,
   Mind me platypus duck.
   All together now!
   Chorus

6. Play your didgeridoo, Blue,
   Play your didgeridoo.
   Keep playing 'til I shoot thro' Blue,
   Play your didgeridoo.
   All together now!
   Chorus

7. Tan me hide when I'm dead, Fred,
   Tan me hide when I'm dead.
   So we tanned his hide when he died Clyde,
   (Spoken:) And that's it hanging on the shed.
   All together now!
   Chorus